More "Fishing Well"

Captain Jeff Waxman

Copyright © 2022 by Jeff Waxman

All rights reserved.
Printed in the United States.

ISBN 978-1-62806-354-7 (print | paperback)

Library of Congress Control Number 2022912263

Published by Salt Water Media
29 Broad Street, Suite 104
Berlin, MD 21811
www.saltwatermedia.com

Cover Page Photograph: First Blue Marlin caught on *Best Revenge* (before we were smart enough to release!) L to R: Dan Young, Charlie Dunn (mate), Bull Tolson (Captain), and Jeff Waxman (author and owner).

Cover design by Salt Water Media

Editing by Bill Cecil

No part of this book may be reproduced or reprinted without the permission of the author.

More "Fishing Well"

In honor of my beloved Eileen

Table of Contents

Author's Note i

Chapter 1: "What the hell is Flamingo?" 1

Chapter 2: Wrong Canyon—Right Fish 5

Chapter 3: No Fish in the Afternoon 8

Chapter 4: An All-Too-Common Cautionary Tale 12

Chapter 5: Winning Tournaments 14

Chapter 6: Exceptional Day, Exceptional Fish 15

Chapter 7: The Two Hour Rule (Credit to Big John) 21

Chapter 8: In Honor of Joe Perez and Billy Black 23

Chapter 9: Catching Cobia in the Gulf with Mike, Mike, and Mike at the Blue Hole 26

Chapter 10: Marlin Fishing? If You Buy the Bait, I'll Buy the Boat! (I Did, He Did!) 29

Chapter 11: Three Good Mates, One Big Fish 32

Chapter 12: Big Blue One—Another Shot 35

Center Photo Section 37

Other Stories 60

Author's Note

This is book three on fishing: short stories, all 100% true. Told as if the crew is sitting at the bar over a beer, or at the dock just hanging out. Hope you enjoy.

- Jeff Waxman

Chapter 1: "What the hell is Flamingo?"

"Cast just over that deep cut, they're in there," suggested the guide. The deep cut was maybe three feet deep, twenty yards from where we were, and we were in about two feet. The live pilchard barely hit the water when it was inhaled by a snook, number 15 or 16, or even more. But I digress.

I wrote the "Old Salts Rule" column for *In The Bite* magazine for several years and thus became friends with the editor, Elliott Stark, who edited my first book. We stayed in contact as he began a fishing newsletter. This past February, he booked a three-day trip out of Islamorada, loved it, called, and suggested I give it a try. And so, based on his suggestion, I contacted Key Hopper Charters and booked my first (way, way in the backcountry) trip. The guide, Mark, and I talked in depth: he suggested a specific day with the correct tide, and we agreed to meet behind World Wide Sportsman at 10:00 am, planning to fish until dark. Far in backcountry with Flamingo (whatever that was) as our ultimate target, his suggested plan.

We met on time and walked to the boat which looked awfully small to me, being mostly an offshore guy. It was a Hells Bay 18-

foot flats boat with a casting platform on the fore deck, a live well behind the tiny helm, a seat in front of the console and a helm seat behind it. The helm might be 20-inch high, teeny grab bar over top, seat in front (half the size of my butt) with a cooler in front of my feet. My hand cooler with lunch and drink crowded the already crowded area for my feet. I assume that some folks used the casting platform, but there's not enough money nor gin for me to get up there!

And so, we get in, get set, and Mark fires up the big Yamaha and we head out. Soon as we clear the area, we are heading West Northwest, deep into the Everglades National Park, in two feet of water over a grassy bottom, 35 knots—and nothing, nothing in sight anywhere. Mark tells me we are heading to Flamingo, which turns out to be a dot of a town on the mainland some forty miles away. As an aside, 35 knots on this pie plate of a boat is way different from 35 knots in a big center console, especially with no hand holds and a teeny seat. Not so sure of this deal, but I'm here, so—

Twenty minutes out and we first slow down, still nothing in sight. We cast to a "deep" cut, using a popping bobber with a rubber shrimp on two-foot leader. Hook up in seconds—small trout; next cast, lady fish; next cast jack, next cast trout—but this time a good-sized lemon shark takes the fish before we get him in. We run ten more minutes to another cut, much the same except this time we catch four snook, one over 26-inch keeper size, but we released. And on the last fish, another lemon tax man collects.

We stop every few minutes, change to pilchards which seem to get bigger fish before a lemon comes to visit (they are pretty much everywhere, maybe 4–6-foot average size, and all hungry).

We begin to see small islands now and again, maybe two feet elevated, full of vegetation. And in three or four places we see weird looking small docks mounted on stakes in the middle of nowhere without houses on them! Put there by park rangers hoping that folks will use them when needed. Best I could tell though, they'd been taken over by birds—everything was covered in inches of white bird droppings and birds were clearly in charge, dozens sitting on each structure, with no intention of moving.

As the tide comes in from the Gulf, we stop at every little island, every tree branch, every (ahem) deep cut. And we catch fish, either a hook up or lost bait on virtually every cast. We stop for lunch about 1:00 pm, and I make the mistake of sitting on the gunwale—luckily, Mark grabs me before I tumble overboard as the teeny boat tilts. Lunch, then more of the same, still miles from Flamingo, but now I at least know what it is! And we catch and we catch, lose one of five or so to the lemons, released everything: fun fishing indeed. It's mid-afternoon, very hot, no breeze and by this time we've caught and released snook, reds, lady fish, trout, jacks, and fought a few sharks. I hook a trout, feels heavier and as it jumps, Marks says, "That's a trophy trout! Any trout over 20-inch in the park in a trophy, let's take it!" So, we do, although it's not so big for most places, it's big for here, nonetheless we ice it down.

It's now maybe 4:00-ish, we have caught maybe 75–100 fish, have one in the box, I am hot (read burning up!) so, gently suggest we "book it for the barn." Mark appears crestfallen, but I assure him it's been a great day; we have exceeded by far any expectations I had, and it's been great. Reluctantly, after a bit of gentle cajoling, we turn back, even having to stop at several spots for the proverbial "one more cast."

We get to the dock just before dark, take another picture of the "trophy trout" (go figure). Mark cleans the fish, bags it, we shake hands (yep, the old way, no fist bump—we're both vaccinated). He tells me that we only fished a partial day, so the charge is minimal (very much so). I get to my home on Cudjoe Key in time for late dinner.

It's been a good day, but, since we never made it to Flamingo, Mark tells me we have to go again!

BTW: Mark Cockerham is guide of Key Hopper Charters in Islamorada. He personally holds several world records and has guided several others to their own world records. He is very good. If you book him and get to Flamingo, please let me know what it's like!

Author and the keeper trout; everything else released. Note the view—nada in any direction!

Chapter 2:
Wrong Canyon—Right Fish!

September 2016, perfect next day forecast for offshore run; a neighbor surf fishing guy wants to go and my buddy who runs a local head boat has the day off. It's a plan. We meet at my boat for a quick run shot at tuna and mahi, pull off dock at 10:00 am—sea flat calm, day perfect. I'm on the helm, neighbor Ron in bolster beside me, Roger in cockpit rigging up—four 30s and a 50 for way, way back line. We set for Baltimore Canyon tip, running 38 knots, gorgeous day. About ten minutes out, I lazily click on the waypoint, but more keeping an eye on neighbor who has never been out sight of land. (Emphasis on the lazily here.) The run should be about an hour and forty minutes to set out.

The day is glorious, boat running fine, neighbor enthralled, and the cockpit set up. But something is just not right. We should be almost there, but we are just in forty fathoms. I decide to actually look carefully, and to my embarrassment, I clicked on the wrong waypoint, and we are heading slightly north of the Baltimore to the South tip of the Wilmington Canyon! Ron has no idea of course, but Roger just laughs, and we continue on to the "wrong" canyon.

Grass everywhere from forty fathoms to overboard as far as you can see. Nonetheless, we set our spread and, while pulling grass constantly, manage to put two gaffers in the boat. Frustrated, we pick up and run ten miles south along the Hundred and the grass lessens up and it becomes fishable, although grass still scattered and it sure looks fishy—fliers, deep blue cobalt water, nice edge. We set out, left long and left flat out, right long goes out, We're in heavy scattered grass, the pin pops. I think it's grass when all of a sudden, the 30 drag begins to sound like tearing canvas—we're hooked up! A Blue jumps 300 yards out. I turn and run parallel with him and bend in a bit so Roger can pick up line. After ten or fifteen frantic minutes, we get the other two lines cleared and stowed and settle into the fight.

My angler Roger is a pro and knows what to do and when to do it, the boat handles easily; seas calm, it shifts into our favor. Ron meanwhile simply looks at me and repeatedly says, "I didn't know fish really got that big. Honest, I didn't." He enjoyed every second in wide-eyed amazement.

We worked the fish on a light drag 10-pound on a 30 standup, Roger in the cockpit and yours truly on the helm. Everything went as it should. We kept the fish within maybe 100 yards and wore her down enough to get a release while she was still strong. The fight lasted maybe an hour and a bit. We called the fish 325–350, average blue marlin for Mid-Atlantic late season, but a trophy on stand up 30, especially on a fun run trip!

By now, it was 4:00 pm, two gaffer mahi in the box and a release, so we picked up for the barn. At just before 6:00, we tied up at Hook'em & Cook'em for fish cleaning. This is where the head boat that Roger runs is docked. Bert, the owner, came out to ask how we did. Roger, being pleased with the day said, "Well, we left at 10:00 am, boated two gaffers, released a blue and tied up at 6:00." Bert, who sees everything at the Marina, looked straight at him and said, "Not so!" Roger looked bit bewildered until Bert smiled at him and said, "Nope. You guys didn't pull out until 10:10."

Some days things go right even they go wrong! Right fish, wrong canyon. Better to be lucky than good.

Chapter 3:
No Fish in the Afternoon!

Anguilla is a beautiful island, twelve miles by three miles, a short six-mile water taxi from St Maarten. It has some of the world's most beautiful beaches—white sand and friendly folks— located dead center between the Atlantic and the Caribbean. We spent four or five years on the island for a month at a time. Famous for the Anguilla Racing Sloop and frequent sailboat races, great food, and island charm. One would expect excellent fishing.

Alas, although Anguilla is situated perfectly for fishing, there appears to be one—and only one—boat available for charter. It is an old 31-foot Bertram, looking its age (mid-1960s) and cruises about 14 knots. Tackle is rudimentary at best and the mate rigs balao by passing the hook through the eye sockets. It's not geared for serious fishing. One boat, that's it. So each year we book the one boat, usually leave dock at 7:00 am, back by noon-ish. And we catch, mahi, yellowfin tuna, and king mackerel.

On our last year in Anguilla another couple wanted to join us, so we set up the charter. However, we decided to go after breakfast so told the boat owner (he and the captain meet each charter) we would like to leave at 10:00. Well, you would think we spoke poorly of their families: a hue and cry began with owner, captain, and even other locals chiming in: "No fish in the afternoon!" Regardless of our protestations, they did not want to hear it. They acted as if we were village idiots. Finally, we reached a conclusion. They agreed to our timing IF we agreed that we would not complain if we came in empty-handed. The trip was on for next day.

We arrived about fifteen minutes early, sat down for coffee, and the waitress immediately repeated the "no fish" warning. So did the captain when he joined us, acting more than a bit annoyed. But we loaded up and plodded offshore, heading for the Atlantic. Our tackle was three ancient 114H Penn Senators, line with visible knots, and a handful of hooks and rust #12 wire

Scale model of the Anguilla skiff

leaders. I rerigged a dozen balao and set up two rigger baits and a shotgun down the middle and sat down to relax. Flat calm seas, 85 degrees, cobalt blue deep water, and as soon as we crossed into maybe forty fathoms, two lines went off. We quickly boated two medium sized kings, maybe 20 pounds each.

As we arrived in the vicinity of the Hundred line, we picked up a nice bull mahi, maybe 25 pounds. As the day went on, we moved in and out of the deep and caught six more kings and one more mahi. We even hooked a big yellowfin, but the line was not up to the task, and we had our only zingpow of the day. It was a beautiful day on the water, and we had ten fish in the box. We paddled our way back to the dock.

And of course waiting there for us (to gloat perhaps?) was the boat owner, several of his friends, and a bunch of hangers-on. By now, the captain had become a believer, so we agreed to say nothing, just to tie up, chat for ten minutes, and then throw the fish on the dock. It worked like a charm.

After ten minutes of being subjected to various comments, we unloaded our fish box. The entourage was stunned and became silent quickly. And then the comments and discussion of "where? how? what?" became the central points. We were local heroes—for the moment—because as the group dispersed, we heard multiple comments on how we had been very fortunate because EVERYONE knows there are "No fish in the afternoon." Go figure.

Perfect ¼ model of Anguilla skiff

Chapter 4:
An All-Too-Common Cautionary Tale

Hudson had a beautiful new custom rig—48 feet and fully loaded with every reasonable option. Top of the line gear, electronics, 30-knot cruise—but Hudson had no friends at the marina. Nobody wanted to fish with him. Too common, but so avoidable.

Hudson was successful: built and sold a high-tech company, and then fishing caught his attention. I met him at the marina where he first arrived with his brandy new 35-foot center console, top brand name and loaded. He hired a local captain to teach him and began to learn fishing well. But noticeably, he always had friends from out of town and a hired mate or captain. Courteous and cordial always, but never really made friends with the folks in the marina. He did well but we all knew that credit went to the "pro" he'd hired. Although he often claimed credit and boasted of his catches.

Fast forward—after three years, Hudson ordered his Carolina Custom rig, which definitely required a bigger slip. And somehow, he managed to get a slip on the fishing dock where both charters and top private rigs were docked. Not easy to do in Ocean City!

At first, Hudson invited a group of top local guys out to fish and to run the trip. They did well, but when fighting a Big Eye, Hudson told the angler to hand him the rod because "it was his boat." Eyebrows were raised, but nothing said. The next trip was also a group of local guys and another incident occurred. It seems as if a small blue marlin crashed a bait while tuna fishing. The fish was not hooked but pulled off in third jump. Nonetheless, they flew a release flag when arriving at the dock. And, left it up!

Now, the local guys were all "busy" when asked to go; so Hudson hired a captain and mate. Local guys also, well respected in the marina. After second trip, they walked out, or he fired them—doesn't matter which though. The stories differed in detail, but the die had been cast—Hudson had unwittingly and unintentionally alienated all of the local guys. In short, he now had no one with whom to fish. And, if he did bring out of town friends, he had no one to work with on the radio nor with whom to share and gain information.

In a fairly short time, Hudson had burned his opportunity to be accepted as part of the group. Now in most circumstances this is unfortunate, but when fishing offshore, miles from land, it even becomes dangerous.

Is there a moral to this story? For sure. Be respectful, tread lightly, and follow the rules of your fishing folks at the local marina. Generally, they are time tested and time honored, and for good reason. Use care and respect.

Stay careful, stay safe, stay respectful, and be courteous!

Chapter 5: Winning Tournaments

Serious tournament folks know this already, nonetheless it bears repeat: tournaments are won THE NIGHT BEFORE! Preparation trumps all else. Sure, luck is a part of the game, but far less than one would expect. If you doubt, just check the top captains listed on "In The Bite" magazine. Over ten years the pattern is crystal clear: the top captains are the top captains, year after year.

"Tournaments are WON the night before!"

Chapter 6:
Exceptional Day, Exceptional Fish

(Reprinted with permission from *Big Game Fishing Journal*)

Well into hour two, it was hard to tell who was starting to tire, our angler, Shane, or the beast some 200 yards out whipping the surface to a froth. Earlier on, one of our crew suggested that "threshers were wimpy sharks." This one was proving him very, very incorrect. It was give and take, with the shark doing most of the taking.

It began as a "what should we fish for today" trip. Mid-May, pretty day, choice of options: canyon for yellowfins, wreck trip for sea bass, deep drop for tiles? The crew was three of us who fish together frequently—Steve, Shane, and yours truly—but we had a fourth guy, Brent, who chimed in that he'd really like to catch a shark! After bit more discussion, we figured a shark trip would be easy. Short run, bucket of chum, and drift three bluefish fillets. It makes for a fun trip, and we can even bottom fish while waiting for a hookup.

We were fishing Steve's boat, a 31-foot Contender Fisharound, fully rigged, room for the crew of four. Generally, my job is the helm (bus driver). Steve runs the cockpit, and Shane and

Brent are our anglers. We picked up a large bucket of chum, a half-dozen fresh bluefish, a half-dozen 10/0 hooks on cable and headed out of Indian River Inlet. The weather was perfect, light and variable out of the SW, seas almost flat. We cruised out at 28 knots, running roughly 30 miles to a set of lumps to the southeast called the Sausages. The perfect place to set up our drift and wait for our target species.

We drilled half dozen holes in the chum bucket, attached it to 8 feet of line and did a troll-speed power drift for maybe 10 minutes, then set our drift, turning the engines such that we drifted beam to northward. We then set three baits, all freshly cut bluefish fillets, maybe 15 to 18 inches long each. The farthest out-line was close to the bottom in 80 feet, second line was approximately halfway down, and the close-in line maybe 10 feet down, all held in place by balloons. We were set.

All rigs were on standup sticks with 50Ws loaded with 50 yards of monofilament top shot on top of 800 yards of 65-pound Spectra braid.

The drift was perfect, about half a knot, beam to, and the baits all looked good. For maybe 5 or 10 minutes we debated maybe bottom fishing, when the close-in balloon popped and the rod loaded up—fish on! Brent was our angler; he had never fought a big fish before but listened to Steve and Shane's coaching. We got our lines in and Brent and the fish settled into the fight.

The fish was fighting like a bulldog, deep short runs, head shaking, giving up line and then running again, but his runs got shorter, and the fish tired fairly quickly. After maybe 20 minutes, Brent had a medium-sized bull shark beside the boat, maybe 150-pound range. Still healthy, we released him to live and fight again. Our day was a success: Brent caught the biggest fish of his life and did a good job in doing so. Success.

Still early in the day, still in the right place, we moved back to our start point, did a quick power chum and set out again. Exact same layout, same baits, but new angler. Shane was up. Brent in relax mode, Steve running the cockpit, me on the helm. Once again, it did not take long, maybe 20 minutes into the second drift, the middle rod went off. Steve took control, setting the hook and handing off to Shane, our angler. If memory serves, Steve offered a belt or harness, but thinking we had another medium-sized bull shark, Shane shook his head and said, "I'll take him without a belt."

A few minutes later, it became obvious to all of us that this was a very different shark indeed. He ran off maybe 400 yards, beating the water to a froth. We realized that we had a thresher—a big thresher! And then he jumped, cleared the water by 5 or 6 feet; we guessed him at 350, maybe a bit better. We got Shane wedged into the transom and I began to work the fish with the boat. I would narrow the gap, trying to keep the fish maybe 100 yards or so off the starboard rear corner. Each time we got close, the shark would run—again and again—and again.

By the end of the first hour neither the fish nor our angler looked to be winning. And it continued, fish runs, work him with the boat and the angler, and he runs again.

By the end of hour two, our angler was showing a bit of wear. The fish continued to run, but runs were shorter, and we began to formulate a plan. We had two guys with big fish experience and a good angler (albeit very tired) on the rod. Our plan was to back down hard, get close enough to wire the fish, hit him with the

Anyone who thinks threshers are wimpy sharks
has never been on the end of a fight like this one.

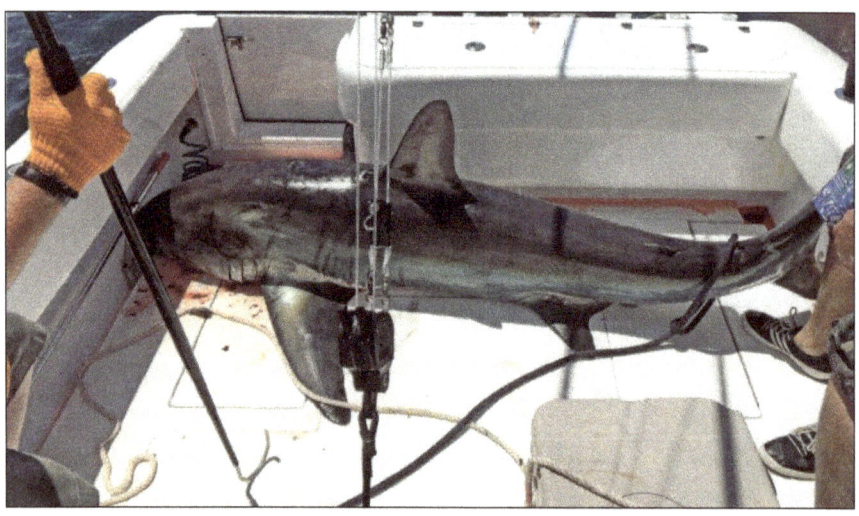

It took more than two hours and four people to flip
this 438-pound thresher into the boat for the trip home.

flyer, and get him cleated off. It was a good plan but depended on Shane holding the fish until Steve could get a couple of wraps on him and at the same time for me to hit him with the flyer, cleat him, and get everybody out of the way of the 10-foot-long tail—which could break an arm!

The plan worked flawlessly, everyone did exactly as told and our prize thresher was hanging on our starboard side—hand gaff holding the head out of the water, flyer deep in the side just ahead of the dorsal. The tail whipped and whipped and slammed against the side of the boat. Once it calmed down, we managed to get a tail wrap around the base of the tail and then a wrap halfway down the tail. We had him! And he was even bigger than we thought—maybe 400! How to get him in the boat?

After several ideas, our boating plan was simple. I grabbed a hand gaff and pulled his head through the transom door. Two guys pulled the flyer rope, and the fourth guy pulled the tail wrap rope, and we flipped him over the motors and into the cockpit! He was in the cockpit, we were all tired—but happy.

We fired up and ran back to the Inlet. He was unloaded with the tackle store crane.

Author sitting on our prize!

He weighed in at 438 pounds. We had had a good day: One angler (Brent) caught his biggest ever and the other angler (Shane) caught his personal best—on standup with no harness.

The best part of the day? We each ended up with over 50 pounds of one of the best-eating fish in the ocean. I steaked out my share, vacuum packed half and had the other half smoked and vacuumed. Exceptional fare resulting from an exceptional trip. Good day, good crew, good plan—it all came together.

A "what-should-we-fish-for" trip turned into a trip full of memories with a personal best shark and plenty of meat for the freezer. (Reprinted with permission of *Big Game Fishing Journal*)

Chapter 7:
The Two Hour Rule
(Credit to Big John)

I am old—really old— but this rule applies to both back in "the day" and now. And damn—it fits.

The theory goes like this. In the 1960s when I began offshore fishing, boats generally cruised between 9 and 10 knots. We fished for bluefish, for bonito, for tuna. And we ran approximately two hours to the "grounds." And we caught fish. Lotsa fish.

In the 1970s, speeds increased to 14–16 knots. And we ran two hours and caught fish!

The 1980s saw speeds increase to 18 knots. We ran two hours—and caught fish. But not as many.

The 1990s, 20 knots, increased horsepower, better hull forms, still ran two hours, and still caught fish. Not so many.

Then in 2000, speeds up to 25 knots, common rail diesels, slippery hulls, bigger rigs—and we ran two hours, and caught fish.

The 2010s, 30 knots needed to keep up, and we ran two hours, and we caught fish, but worked harder and fished longer for them.

Now in the 2020s, running 35 knots and some 40. Bigger, better hulls and engines (and fuel capacity) and we run two hours to different canyons and structure. We catch fish, not so many now.

The summary? Consider the data and the story tells itself!

Chapter 8:
In honor of Joe Perez and Billy Black

The rig: My buddy Joe's 36-foot *Hatteras*, out of Oregon Inlet, NC. Early May 1978. Joe at the helm, yours truly the mate.

The crew: Joe, me, Billy Black, and my girlfriend—her first offshore run.

The day: May 10, and we pull off the dock at 5:00 am sharp, headed for the Point, north side by the 800 line. Joe loafs us along at 18 knots, the ride smooth, sunrise gorgeous. Looks like a good start.

There had been a good run of medium yellowfin tuna through May, but it has slacked off a bit as waters warmed. Catches were down from limits daily to half dozen per boat, which would have been fine for us.

Tuna baits went out at 6:20 am, seas running 3–4 feet, lazy swells, nine baits out, all running good. We trolled at 6.5–7 knots, working from the 50 to the 200 and back. We changed several baits, lengthened and shortened a few, changed speeds a touch—no love yet. The radio traffic matched the slowness of the start, but high hopes. And at 9:15, the shotgun (down the middle, way back, on a 50 with #15 single strand wire leader) went off—the hit looking like a locomotive had been dropped on the bait. It began.

We cleared the lines, girlfriend was in the chair, Joe handling the boat, running parallel to the fish. We realized this was not a school class yellowfin, not by a long shot. Joe kept us couple hundred yards off until the fish settled a bit, then as we got closer, the fish sounded. Two hours of give and take (mostly give), no color, no sighting yet—but this fish was a stud! Finally, two and a half hours later, Joe called color. Big tuna! The fish was getting tired, girlfriend did great job, gaining inches at a time. I had the flyer rigged and cleated off, 25 feet of ½-inch line. We were ready!

She fought her fish well (curse words omitted—they don't count) in the chair with good form. Me on one side, Billy guiding the chair, and finally had a good gaff shot off the starboard side. Perfect hit deep in shoulder, I expected the fish to roll over. He did not, rather he dragged my 260 pounds across the transom hanging on, afraid to dump the wire and lose fish to a kink. He dragged me to the port side and started toward the bow, Joe yelling to Billy, "Get the straight big hook gaff!" as he came almost to plane. I managed one more wrap, than another, Billy got the second gaff in deep, the fish tail slapped the hull side, bled a ton, then turned on his side. We had our prize—finally, at the start of hour three!

Well, Joe, Billy, and girlfriend outdid themselves on this trip. Great company, great day, great fish, lotsa laughs, and wonderful hours sitting on the bridge with Joe. The fish was the biggest tuna we had ever seen, guessed at 260 pounds, but TBD. We caught three others, all 35–40-pound school fish, then left an hour early for the weigh-in. Well, by the time we got the fish up on the scales (242 pounds), took couple pix and drank a few cold ones, the fleet arrived.

The entire trip was a success, even more so when Captain BC walked up (beer in left hand and ice cream sandwich in the other), looked our fish and said, "Y'all boys done good. First Big Eye of the season and she's a big un." Well, once he'd walked away, we all looked each other, then at the fish—none of us had even heard of a Big Eye tuna then! We all thought it was an overgrown yellowfin, until we really looked at the eyes and body shape. Yep, our first (of many over the years) Big Eye tuna.

Girlfriend had one helluva start. In her considered view, it was the Best Fish—ever!

Joe and Billy have both passed, very glad they were there; couldn't have caught the fish without both! They are missed ….

Chapter 9: Catching Cobia in the Gulf with Mike, Mike, and Mike at the Blue Hole

Young Mike had worked for years as a mate in Delaware; Big Mike, and Uncle Mike had all met at the family condo in January 2019 for a week of fishing in the Keys. By now, Young Mike had earned his ticket and was running charters out of Duck Key (just north of Marathon). And through his contacts he had gained the numbers for the Blue Hole, 55 miles into the Gulf from Duck. All of the Mikes were excellent fisherman. Young Mike caught the live bait, and I was fortunate enough to be invited!

The boat was a beautiful 31-foot Cape Horn, fully outfitted and powered by twin 300 Yammies— comfortable and fast! The run out was bumpy, took two hours or so, but that was just the beginning of this new adventure. Seems as if the bottom is exactly 42 feet—no structure, and nothing of note. Until we got there. Three or four boats were tightly anchored over an area maybe

Cobia in the Gulf

the footprint of a small building. Since we knew nothing of the details, we anchored about 150 feet away and begin to cast our live (large) grunts for bait. Hour one, bites zero!

Finally, Young Mike had a call from one of the anchored boats, a charter friend telling us to join "the party," anchor within feet of the other boats at the edge of the hole, with fish on every cast! So, we pulled up and joined the tight little fleet and cast to the hole—85–100 feet deep surrounded by 42 feet of flats. And we caught cobes—lotsa cobes—18 in total! Lines tangled, folks laughed, spirits were high, and fishing was great. Our fish went from 35 to 56 inches; we kept our limit and began to release. By now, the little fleet was maybe 8 or 9 boats, and all were catching and enjoying, tangles and all. Great party.

Meanwhile, a boat beside us set up a bent butt 80 in rod holder, dropped a lively to the bottom and in seconds the rod doubled over! We watched the fight for fifteen or twenty minutes until a mid-sized goliath grouper was released unharmed. From our vantage point, based on the size of his fins, we guessed him at maybe 130–150 pounds. Quite a fish.

Soon it was mid-day, seas had laid down, and we were out of bait. Time to head for the barn. Young Mike drove as we cruised home at 42 knots, relaxed and happy. But the best was yet to come. We tied up and Big Mike immediately went to make Bloody Marys, Uncle Mike and I sat on the bench as Young Mike cleaned eight cobes (two per), packed them in ice, and after reliving a great day, we left to grill our prize cobia steaks for dinner.

Thanks Mikes, for inviting me. Owe you a fishing trip!

Chapter 10:
Marlin Fishing? If you Buy the Bait, I'll Buy the Boat! (I Did, He Did!)

Mid '80s, started hunting with couple of new guys and while talking about fish out of Oregon Inlet, that comment was made out loud. We laughed, but Dan was serious and offered to buy a 27-foot Aquasport with twin outboards and tow it to NC for a blue marlin trip. He did and we did. Ahh, hindsight is always better!

We met at the dock, I supplied all but the boat: tackle, rods and reels, flying and straight gaffs—everything. Dan picked his crew; I knew them but not well enough. Dan, his buddy Ed, and Jack (straight from a vasectomy the day before). We set out and 35 miles to the Point before we put Dan on the helm; I set out five baits: a Spanish, a swimming mullet, and three horse balao—all on 50s. Calm, boats in every direction, pilot whales around, cobalt water. It looked perfect.

Couple of white ones released, couple schools of dolphin, couple of tuna, but the radio was fairly quiet. And then, the Spanish disappeared in a huge splash (someone toss a car at it?). I grabbed the rod, did a long, long drop back, started to reel—blue marlin hooked up!

Quickly put Dan in the rod and grabbed the helm to run with the fish as he tail-walked and greyhounded for starters. Dan had no idea what he was doing; tried to reel at exactly wrong time and after maybe 15 minutes said, "I'm done! Somebody please take the rod."

Not what I expected but then—

Ed took the rod, harnessed in and doing great (only by comparison) until sweat ran down his face and he too quit! Jack is up. As he's holding the rod to get set up, he screams in pain. "Help, please, my balls hurt badly". What had I done pray tell?

Well there are boats all around us, and I knew most of them were enjoying the small-boat, half-assed crew trying to get the fish—sorta like watching a monkey try to screw a football. Radio alive with laughter.

No option, fish getting tired now, fight mostly in the surface and close in. Managed to work boat toward fish, get close enough for release when Dan yells, "I want to mount this fish." Change gears, grab flyer as the crew moves as far away as 27 feet will allow.

Fish gaffed, cleated off, they help get it into the boat. About 1:30, time to head in before the fleet, fuel up, and get mount written up. All done; disaster free (so far). Mount put into freezer at Fishing Center, truck comes for pick up in a week.

Dinner, drinks, jokes and laughs (many at Jack's tender balls), sleep in, breakfast and the boys and boat head back up the road. All good! One trip, blue marlin, calm day, fun mostly, until—

The taxidermist (Pete) called me at home two weeks later. Well, it seems that Dan (methinks his wife perhaps?) upon finding out the total cost of the mount, wrote a check that bounced—and refused to make it good! Go figure.

Well, MY MOUNT, including shipping, crating, and discount, came to $1100—as if I wanted another mount!

In conclusion: I have not hunted with the boys since. Oh, and the fish weighed 275.

Live and learn!

Chapter 11:
Three Good Mates, One Big Fish!

Early May 2010—early for offshore—bottom fishing still slow, everyone bored. Three good mates—Adam, Steve, and Brad—had no charters and bored. They're young guys (Eileen calls them my Boy Scouts) and good friends; we contemplate the day. What to do? We reach a plan.

We will go fishing for thresher sharks: great fight, good on the table, and close in early season—and they get big. We buy a five-gallon bucket of chum, load three 50s into my 35-foot center console and head out about 8 miles to the B buoy, straight off Indian River inlet.

We set up chum, did mile or so slow power chumming, then stop and get rigs ready—16/0 hooks on 300 pound 15-foot mono leader. Plan is to do slow drift with three baits out—deep nearest, middle with balloon maybe 30 yards out, and ballooned bottom rig just above 85-foot bottom. We relax and get stand up belt ready. The plan is to boat the fish if we get hookup.

Three minutes go by, still in get-ready mode and mid-depth balloon disappears; we get a look at a thresher tail maybe five feet out of the water, thrashing then disappears. Looked big. Adam grabs the gloves and says, "Jeff, I'll wire the fish, you have the helm. Let's get him." We clear the other two lines as half the spool disappears—Steve on the rod, belt on and ready.

The fish runs and runs and runs some more. Finally, we get some line back and the fish jumps clear of the water; every bit of 700 but more likely 800 pounds. Threshers do run big—state record approximately 650—but clearly this fish was very, very big. And whipping the water with his tail. Once we saw the fish, Adam says, "This fish is scary! You've had big fish experience. How 'bout you wiring? I can gaff." And we agree. But long way to go before we face a landing, if at all. Threshers use their tail to disable their prey before devouring, hence the tail is as long as the body, best guess maybe 15–16 feet total size—big!

The fish was strong and clearly not tiring, Steve was on light leather belt with Teflon gimbal. And he was tired after close to two hours, all fought with the fish out maybe 200 or so yards. So, we did the switch; Brad on the rod. Both Steve and Brad are experienced and damned good anglers; but two more hours and no progress yet.

Adam's turn on the rod. I dared to increase drag a touch to maybe 18–20 pounds, hoping it would help. It did but only a bit, so I decided to try and get closer using boat power. We managed after half-hour to get the fish to maybe fifty yards out. But the fish kept the distance constant and stayed the same distance for another hour plus. Now, we have three tired anglers and nowhere close to boating the fish. We decided that: 1–we will not use a rod holder to help, and 2–we will adjust drag cautiously until we either win or lose him.

It was time to up the ante.

Adam still on the rod, fish still fifty yards out, drag now at 22 pounds—no progress. We adjust another two pounds—no progress. Anglers tired, fish appears to stay strong. We discuss again: what to do!

We decided to go for broke. Plan to use the boat to get close enough for a shot with flyer and to add two more pounds drag. Well, half the plan worked, drag tightened, no gain on the fish. The mates discussed; plan now is for sure a home run or strike out. I donned gloves, readied the gaff, and powered to maybe 20 feet from the fish. It looked even bigger! Per the plan, Adam tightened drag yet again to maybe 25–30 pounds, and we gain another few feet.

And then, of course, the inevitable happens—we lose him to a break in the line (50-pound mono). Everyone did their job; everyone was on their game. So what happened?

The answer was clear. We used a 15-foot leader, but the threshers tail was hitting the main line on every run and, after six or more hours, the main was chafed and was no longer 50-pound test. After feeling the chafed line, I was surprised that it lasted as long as it did. The answer was clear.

Sometimes the fish wins. And in a strange way, I was happy for him to win. He earned it.

Chapter 12:
Big Blue One—Another Shot!

July 1980, Oregon Inlet, NC; we're fishing my buddy's boat, fun trip planned. Yours truly on the helm on 28-foot Bertram, Gibbs running the cockpit (first time), and his girlfriend and her friend were the anglers. Both girls very attractive. We pulled out late, the day looked to be a scorcher—flat and still. And before we got to the 50, both girls were wearing only bikini bottoms! Gonna be interesting for sure!

After about an hour, we find a good solid weed line, troll until we find the dolphin school. Pull in the rigs, set up to chum and get out two dink rigs. Gibbs doing really well, bring in fish, rebait, and do it again. The school was mainly small but keepers, maybe 5 to 7 each and staying with the hooked fish—we're doing good. I called over two charter boats to join the party (we really do that at Oregon Inlet. Really!).

GulfStream came over and set up nearby as did the Deepwater. All going good until—

A big blue one came out of the water and grabbed one of our hooked dolphin. It was an awesome sight, fish beautiful and the fight started slowly. We got Gibbs in the chair, harnessed but we knew the odds were with the fish using a dink rod. We managed carefully to move out a bit, but the fish was not fighting as expected, in fact I doubt that the 4/0 hook was bothering him. Until we were maybe 100 yards from the other boats.

The girls were ecstatic (me too) and put in an 8-track tape of the long version of "All I Need is the Air that I Breathe." Unbelievable in every way! Blue one hooked but seemed to be giving up easily. Two beautiful young women half-dressed on either side of the chair, Eagles blaring out song at full volume. It actually occurred to me: "Can it be any better?" I decide then that if my time on earth was to be short, take me now!

But, the idyllic scenario changed in an instant. The fish (350–400-ish) decided to change the game and greyhounded across maybe 150 yards (almost landing in GulfStream's cockpit!). He jumped through the weed line, did a hard ninety-degree turn, and the hook pulled.

Well, at least I had a long life ahead!

Photo Section

50-pound Cobia off Indian Inlet July 2018—Steve and Dr. Pat

Back in the day—Oregon Inlet 1974—546 pounds

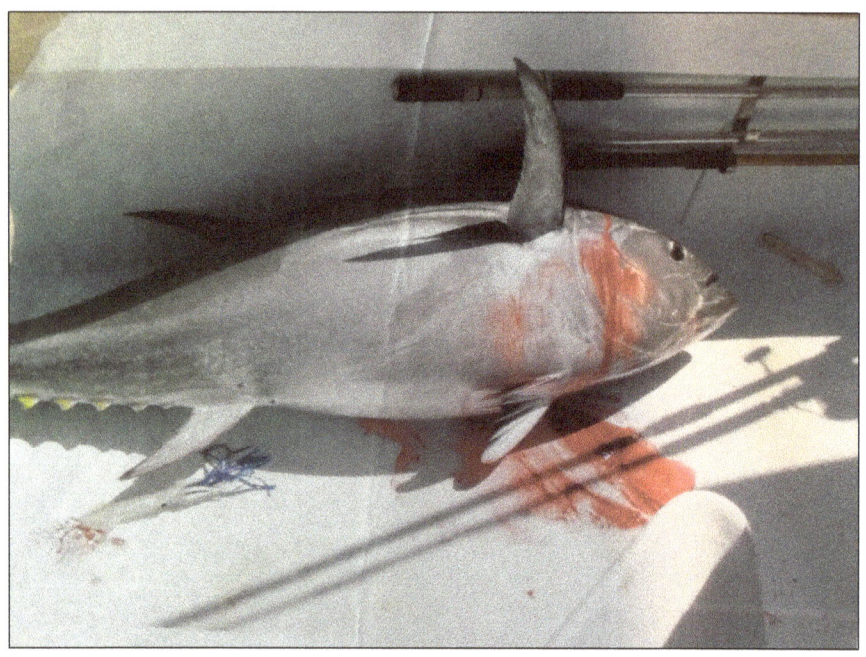

Big Bluefin—Oregon Inlet 2012

Chris TF crossing to Walkers Cay 1974.

Captain Bull Tolson on my boat Best Revenge

48-inch Cobia caught in the Chesapeake Bay August 2017.
Caught eleven that day.

Dr. Pat fighting four tiles at once—Indian River July 2018. Top fish weighed in at 18 pounds.

Dr. Pat with Sailfish

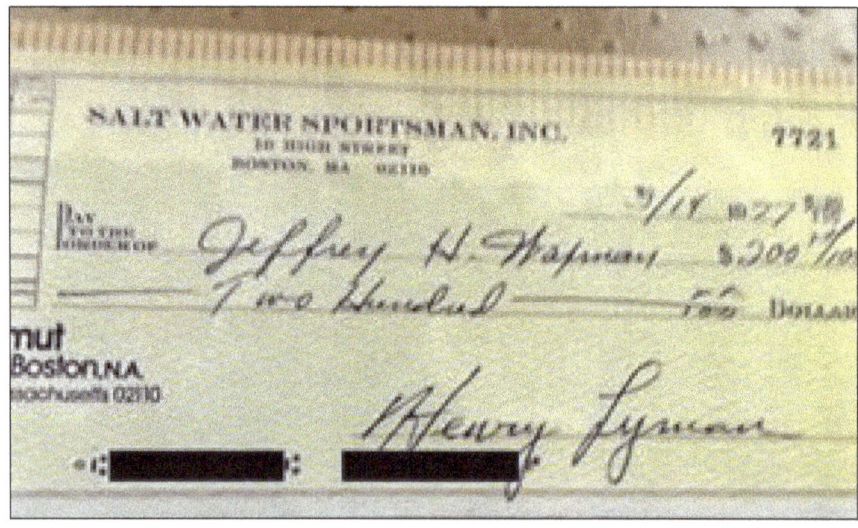

First article published—June 1977—SWS

First blue caught on Foxy Lady, 1974.
30' Tournament Fish

Eight-foot lemon shark on 25-pound drag and still running.
Cudjoe Key — March 2020

First tilefish on SeaFlame. 19.9 pounds. First drop, first try for tiles!

Good day for tuna. Oregon Inlet, April 2019. Yours truly. Tough fish on 50 wides.

Good day tile fishing. Indian River 2019.

Swordfish being steaked out. 316 lbs.

King macs. Cudjoe Key, Florida. Largest was 45 pounds.

White Marlin Open 2007 I believe. Boat hit deadhead.
We got 5 head and much gear off the boat. Ocean City, MD.

Nice bull dolphin caught in 1972, Oregon Inlet.

Small blue one came up dead. Foxy Lady, Oregon Inlet 1976.

Ready-to-serve fresh caught tuna "crudite".

Swordfishing out of Islamorada. Author and Nick Stanczyk. Released five that trip, between 100–150 pounds.

They're in the boat—all four, hand-cranked. Dr. Pat on a roll.

Took two buddies on 37-foot O'Neal Brillfisher. Oregon Inlet, 1975.

Took Eric Burnley, sportswriter, to the deep. Nice load of tile. July 2017. RUFF ride home! Author, Pat, Steve, Shane, and Eric.

2019 White Marlin Open tuna. Held first place until last day. Dr. Pat, son Patrick, mate Rodney, and author. Ocean City, Maryland.

Other Stories

Some of the best stories heard from friends on the trip offshore. With attribution, of course.

Mike and the Mako

Good friend Mike loved shark fishing and often booked charters for makos. After a few years of successful trips, Mike and friend John figured they were ready to give it a try on their own. (Spoiler alert—they weren't.)

So they convinced John's dad to loan them his new 27-foot Grady walkaround. They fueled up, loaded bait and ice and fishing tackle. They were now ready. Off they head to the PoorMans, set up chum line and baited three rigs with bluefish filet on 14/0 circle hooks and 10-foot heavy leader (single strand #15 wire); one deep, one mid, and one surface—all with balloons to maintain depth.

And in fifteen minutes, surface balloon moves against current, then pops—fish on! One jump shows a medium mako, maybe 200 pounds. One more jump, a bit of thrashing, and the fish comes in easily. They get it to boatside, still calm, and having no flyer, gaff it with large gaff and quickly get it into the boat, whereupon it did exactly what makos do—destroyed everything on the deck. Mike and John managed to not get bitten nor tail-whipped but did spend two entire hours laying on the hardtop, clinging on for dear life. Only after they were certain the mako had expired did they venture down.

The lesson? Priceless! The cost to repair the boat? Many thousands of dollars!

Green and not-dead-yet sharks MUST be left in the water until: 1) gaffed, 2) tail-wrapped, 3) dragged backwards for an hour, and 4) make absolute certain shark is dead dead before attempting to bring it aboard. Pay heed, please!

— As told by Captain Mike Herrman

Marvin

My younger daughter Jessica is my hunting and fishing buddy, but over time she ended up in Park City, Utah, whilst I was living in Delaware and fishing three or more times per week. And so, I schemed to try to convince her to move East.

At the time, she was caretaker of a horse barn on ten acres of land at the edge of a mountain, fenced with a small pond near the outer edge. She took care of the horses and lived in an apartment over top—idyllic and peaceful, with wildlife around constantly which, being an animal kid, she loved.

And then, in early spring she came upon a moose calf near the pond, clearly abandoned by the mother (assuming she had twins and only cared for the stronger one as is typical). Well, Jessi adopted said calf, took over his care and fed him until he grew up and was able to fend for himself. But he imprinted on her as his mother, following her everywhere, even ducking his head to go into the barn to hay the horses. She named him Marvin and cared for him for several years—even spraying chartreuse paint on both his sides to spell "PET" so he wouldn't be shot by hunters. He slept under her deck and grew to be a world class Shiras bull moose—all the while hanging with Jessica and the horses inside the ten-acre fence.

Fast forward to me explaining what a great idea it would be to move East. It sure made sense to me, but after the discussion, and in an offhand way, Jessi says, "And who will take care of

Marvin?" Marvin, the full-grown, 1200-pound beast with world class rack—and Jessi worries about who will take care of him? Go figure.

It took three years, but after Marvin had acclimated and was less "Jessi-dependent," Jessi and husband moved East! Marvin— the bull moose with the temperament of a Labrador puppy!

— Attribution to Jessi Waxman

Free Thanksgiving Turkey

Late 70s, fishing Chesapeake Bay with Bill Cain, and he told the story of his free turkey. Bill grew up in a rural area in Kentucky where several turkey farms existed to raise annual turkey crops for Thanksgiving.

Well, one fishing day, Bill and his buddies came up with a plan to "liberate" a turkey for each of their families, at the expense of a local farmer of course. And so the plan emerged: head for the farm with the most turkeys the farthest from the farmhouse, in the middle of night on cloudy low-moon night. So, they did. They pulled up beside the 8-foot-high fence at the far end very slowly, lights off. There were thousands of turkeys, all quiet and appearing to be asleep. Bill was to scale the fence, grab three turkeys, wring their neck, toss each bird over to his friends, then climb back over to the car. It didn't exactly work that way.

As soon as Bill hit the ground, he realized that: 1) the ground was really four or more inches of turkey crap, more slippery than axle grease; and 2) every turkey within a hundred foot radius knew he was there; and 3) every single one attacked him with beaks, claws, and flapping wings! Bill fell to the ground, covered with turkey crap and attacked by dozens of flailing, gobbling turkeys. It was a pure debacle. Bill tried to stand, lost his glasses, had his shirt ripped to pieces, one shoe lost, and feverishly tried unsuccessfully to get back out of the turkey yard when all the lights on every pole came on, the farmer's truck came screaming to a halt with said farmer and son jumping out—each carrying a shotgun!

Figuring they had a fox problem, the farmers were not expecting to see what they saw and fell to their knees in laughter! Two young guys hiding under their car, with Bill being attacked by and ripped to shreds by the turkeys. It had to be one helluva sight to see. The farmers put shotguns away, shooed the turkeys off Bill, and helped him over the fence—bloody, ripped clothes, one shoe, and hugely embarrassed. The other two? Sheepish would be an understatement.

And the farmers? After thoroughly chastising the boys with threats of being shot for grand larceny, the farmers gave each boy a free turkey, saying it was worth the laughs!

— Attribution to Bill Cain

The Cats on Fire!

Heading offshore one day, my BFF told this story. It seems that one of his nurses decided to hold a romantic dinner for her husband's birthday, setting the table with flowers and champagne. She placed long-burning candles strategically throughout the bedroom with big plans: dinner, followed by romance in the boudoir, then deep sleep—what's not to like?

Dinner was superb, perfectly served, followed by champagne and custard dessert. After which—as per plan—they retired to the bedroom where the strategically placed candles cast a romantic glow. It was perfect. And as they began to enjoy the night to its fullest, she suddenly exclaimed: "The cat's on fire!"

To which the husband replied: "All right, honey."

She yelled louder: "The cat's really on fire!"

His reply? "No worries, I'm on it!"

Well, it seems that the elderly, half-blind cat followed them into the bedroom, whereupon he brushed against a candle and his old fur caught fire! Yep, the real cat was really on fire!

The romance was scrapped, cat taken to emergency vet and survived, albeit somewhat the worse for wear and "fur-less" on part of one side.

— Attribution to Dr. Pat

The author's fleet… from the firstest….to the lastest!

- 8' Hydroplane
- 14' Trojan Sea Queen
- 18' Chris Craft
- 17' Sea Ray
- 18' Sea Ray
- 23' Formula Cuddy
- 23' Formula center console
- 25' Marauder
- 16' Jet
- 30' TF
- 36' Harris
- 47' Davis
- 52' Sportsman (partner)
- 17' Whaler
- 21' Trophy
- 30' Donzi center console
- 35' Donzi center console
- 24' Privateer
- 25' Grady

Author's 35' Donzi center console

Best Revenge — Oregon Inlet, 1981

Marauder — Chesapeake Bay, 1973

After You — Indian River, 2006

www.ingramcontent.com/pod-product-compliance
Lightning Source LLC
Chambersburg PA
CBHW050817090426
42736CB00022B/3485